CRANE CLASSICS

SHAKESPEARE
SELECTED SONNETS

CRANE CLASSICS

Shakespeare

Selected Sonnets

Selected and introduced by
Anthony Eyre

MOUNT ORLEANS
PRESS

Crane Classics Poetry Series
Series editor: Anthony Eyre

This collection first published in 2020 by
Mount Orleans Press
23 High Street, Cricklade SN6 6AP
https://anthonyeyre.com

CIP data for this title are available from the British Library

Typography and book production by Anthony Eyre

ISBN 978-1-912945-20-7

Printed in the UK
by the Short Run Press Ltd
Exeter

Frontispiece:

William Shakespeare
Leisure Hour Magazine, 1864

CONTENTS

SHAKE-SPEARES

SONNETS.

Neuer before Imprinted.

AT LONDON
By *G. Eld* for *T. T.* and are
to be folde by *William Aſpley.*
1609.

INTRODUCTION

S HAKESPEARE'S *SONNETS* were first published in 1609, the poet's 45th year, a period during which he is thought to have been writing his later plays, such as *Pericles, Cymbeline* and *The Winter's Tale*. They are the last of his non-dramatic works to be published. But – and this is consistent with everything we might speculate about the *Sonnets* – this information does not lead to much in the way of knowledge or understanding. We know that two of the sonnets, 138 and 144, had been included in a collection of verse (*The Passionate Pilgrim*) published ten years before in 1599. We can see that the collection divides thematically, with a section devoted to the 'Fair Youth' (1-126), and then the introduction of the 'Dark Lady' (127-152). The last two sonnets in the collection stand alone in being rather formulaic renditions of a traditional conceit threading through the story of Cupid and the theft of his 'love-kindling fire'.

Further head scratching has been caused to scholars by the dedication (reproduced overleaf) to 'Mr. W.H.' WH has been identified most typically as either William Herbert, Earl of Pembroke, or Henry Wriothesley, Earl of Southampton; and by some (perhaps out of desperation) as 'William Himself', i.e. Shakespeare. The dedication is in fact signed not by Shakespeare, but by TT, Thomas Thorpe, the publisher, who had also published Ben Jonson and Christopher Marlowe. What, after all this, is undeniable is the claim made for the Fair Youth in various ways in different sonnets:

My love shall in my verse ever live young.

TO.THE.ONLIE.BEGETTER.OF.
THESE.INSVING.SONNETS.
Mr. W. H. ALL.HAPPINESSE.
AND.THAT.ETERNITIE.
PROMISED.

BY.

OVR.EVER-LIVING.POET.

WISHETH.

THE.WELL-WISHING.
ADVENTVRER.IN.
SETTING.
FORTH.

T. T.

FROM FAIREST creatures we desire increase,
That thereby beauty's rose might never die,
But as the riper should by time decease,
His tender heir might bear his memory:
But thou, contracted to thine own bright eyes,
Feed'st thy light's flame with self-substantial fuel,
Making a famine where abundance lies,
Thyself thy foe, to thy sweet self too cruel:
Thou that art now the world's fresh ornament,
And only herald to the gaudy spring,
Within thine own bud buriest thy content,
And, tender churl, mak'st waste in niggarding:
    Pity the world, or else this glutton be—
    To eat the world's due, by the grave and thee.

2

WHEN FORTY winters shall besiege thy brow,
And dig deep trenches in thy beauty's field,
Thy youth's proud livery so gaz'd on now,
Will be a totter'd weed of small worth held:
Then being ask'd, where all thy beauty lies,
Where all the treasure of thy lusty days,
To say within thine own deep sunken eyes
Were an all-eating shame, and thriftless praise.
How much more praise deserv'd thy beauty's use,
If thou couldst answer: 'This fair child of mine
Shall sum my count, and make my old excuse,'—
Proving his beauty by succession thine!
      This were to be new made when thou art old,
      And see thy blood warm when thou feel'st it cold.

3

LOOK IN thy glass and tell the face thou viewest
Now is the time that face should form another,
Whose fresh repair if now thou not renewest
Thou dost beguile the world, unbless some mother.
For where is she so fair whose unear'd womb
Disdains the tillage of thy husbandry?
Or who is he so fond will be the tomb
Of his self-love, to stop posterity?
Thou art thy mother's glass and she in thee
Calls back the lovely April of her prime;
So thou through windows of thine age shalt see,
Despite of wrinkles, this thy golden time.
    But if thou live, remembered not to be,
    Die single and thine image dies with thee.

4

UNTHRIFTY LOVELINESS, why dost thou spend
Upon thy self thy beauty's legacy?
Nature's bequest gives nothing, but doth lend,
And being frank she lends to those are free:
Then, beauteous niggard, why dost thou abuse
The bounteous largess given thee to give?
Profitless usurer, why dost thou use
So great a sum of sums, yet canst not live?
For having traffic with thy self alone,
Thou of thy self thy sweet self dost deceive:
Then how when nature calls thee to be gone—
What acceptable audit canst thou leave?
　　Thy unused beauty must be tomb'd with thee,
　　Which, used, lives th'executor to be.

5

THOSE HOURS that with gentle work did frame
 The lovely gaze where every eye doth dwell,
Will play the tyrants to the very same
And that unfair which fairly doth excel:
For never-resting time leads summer on
To hideous winter, and confounds him there;
Sap checked with frost, and lusty leaves quite gone,
Beauty o'er-snowed and bareness everywhere:
Then were not summer's distillation left
A liquid prisoner pent in walls of glass,
Beauty's effect with beauty were bereft,
Nor it, nor no remembrance what it was.
    But flowers distill'd, though they with winter meet,
    Leese but their show: their substance still lives sweet.

7

Lo, in the orient when the gracious light
Lifts up his burning head, each under eye
Doth homage to his new-appearing sight,
Serving with looks his sacred majesty;
And having climb'd the steep-up heavenly hill,
Resembling strong youth in his middle age,
Yet mortal looks adore his beauty still,
Attending on his golden pilgrimage:
But when from highmost pitch, with weary car,
Like feeble age he reeleth from the day,
The eyes, ('fore duteous) now converted are
From his low tract, and look another way:
    So thou, thyself outgoing in thy noon
    Unlooked on diest unless thou get a son.

8

M USIC TO hear, why hear'st thou music sadly?
Sweets with sweets war not, joy delights in joy:
Why lov'st thou that which thou receiv'st not gladly,
Or else receiv'st with pleasure thine annoy?
If the true concord of well-tunèd sounds,
By unions married, do offend thine ear,
They do but sweetly chide thee, who confounds
In singleness the parts that thou shouldst bear:
Mark how one string, sweet husband to another,
Strikes each in each by mutual ordering;
Resembling sire and child and happy mother,
Who, all in one, one pleasing note do sing:
    Whose speechless song being many, seeming one,
    Sings this to thee: 'Thou single wilt prove none.'

9

Is it for fear to wet a widow's eye,
That thou consum'st thy self in single life?
Ah! if thou issueless shalt hap to die,
The world will wail thee like a makeless wife;
The world will be thy widow and still weep
That thou no form of thee hast left behind,
When every private widow well may keep
By children's eyes, her husband's shape in mind:
Look what an unthrift in the world doth spend
Shifts but his place, for still the world enjoys it;
But beauty's waste hath in the world an end,
And kept unused the user so destroys it.
    No love toward others in that bosom sits
    That on himself such murd'rous shame commits.

For shame deny that thou bear'st love to any,
Who for thy self art so unprovident!
Grant if thou wilt, thou art belov'd of many,
But that thou none lov'st is most evident:
For thou art so possess'd with murderous hate,
That 'gainst thy self thou stick'st not to conspire,
Seeking that beauteous roof to ruinate
Which to repair should be thy chief desire:
Oh change thy thought, that I may change my mind!
Shall hate be fairer lodg'd than gentle love?
Be as thy presence is, gracious and kind,
Or to thyself at least kind-hearted prove:
    Make thee another self for love of me,
    That beauty still may live in thine or thee.

As fast as thou shalt wane so fast thou grow'st
In one of thine from that which thou departest;
And that fresh blood which youngly thou bestow'st,
Thou mayst call thine when thou from youth convertest.
Herein lives wisdom, beauty, and increase;
Without this, folly, age, and cold decay:
If all were minded so, the times should cease,
And threescore year would make the world away.
Let those whom nature hath not made for store—
Harsh, featureless, and rude—barrenly perish:
Look, whom she best endow'd, she gave the more;
Which bounteous gift thou shouldst in bounty cherish:
    She carved thee for her seal, and meant thereby,
    Thou shouldst print more, not let that copy die.

1 2

WHEN I do count the clock that tells the time,
   And see the brave day sunk in hideous night;
When I behold the violet past prime,
And sable curls, all silvered o'er with white;
When lofty trees I see barren of leaves,
Which erst from heat did canopy the herd,
And summer's green all girded up in sheaves,
Borne on the bier with white and bristly beard:
Then of thy beauty do I question make,
That thou among the wastes of time must go,
Since sweets and beauties do themselves forsake
And die as fast as they see others grow;
   And nothing 'gainst Time's scythe can make defence
   Save breed, to brave him when he takes thee hence.

OH THAT you were your self! but, love, you are
No longer yours, than you your self here live:
Against this coming end you should prepare,
And your sweet semblance to some other give:
So should that beauty which you hold in lease
Find no determination; then you were
Yourself again after yourself's decease,
When your sweet issue your sweet form should bear.
Who lets so fair a house fall to decay,
Which husbandry in honour might uphold
Against the stormy gusts of winter's day
And barren rage of death's eternal cold?
     Oh none but unthrifts, dear my love you know:
     You had a father: let your son say so.

16

Bᴜᴛ ᴡʜᴇʀᴇꜰᴏʀᴇ do not you a mightier way
Make war upon this bloody tyrant Time,
And fortify your self in your decay
With means more blessèd than my barren rhyme?
Now stand you on the top of happy hours,
And many maiden gardens, yet unset,
With virtuous wish would bear you living flowers,
Much liker than your painted counterfeit:
So should the lines of life that life repair,
Which this (Time's pencil or my pupil pen)
Neither in inward worth nor outward fair
Can make you live yourself in eyes of men.
  To give away yourself keeps your self still,
    And you must live drawn by your own sweet skill.

WHO WILL believe my verse in time to come?
      If it were fill'd with your most high deserts—
Though yet heaven knows it is but as a tomb
Which hides your life and shows not half your parts—
If I could write the beauty of your eyes,
And in fresh numbers number all your graces,
The age to come would say: 'This poet lies;
Such heavenly touches ne'er touch'd earthly faces.'
So should my papers, yellow'd with their age,
Be scorn'd, like old men of less truth than tongue,
And your true rights be term'd a poet's rage
And stretchèd metre of an antique song:
      But were some child of yours alive that time,
      You should live twice—in it and in my rhyme.

18

SHALL I compare thee to a summer's day?
Thou art more lovely and more temperate:
Rough winds do shake the darling buds of May,
And summer's lease hath all too short a date:
Sometime too hot the eye of heaven shines,
And often is his gold complexion dimm'd,
And every fair from fair sometime declines,
By chance or nature's changing course untrimm'd:
But thy eternal summer shall not fade,
Nor lose possession of that fair thou ow'st,
Nor shall Death brag thou wander'st in his shade,
When in eternal lines to time thou grow'st,
      So long as men can breathe, or eyes can see,
      So long lives this, and this gives life to thee.

Devouring Time, blunt thou the lion's paws,
And make the earth devour her own sweet brood;
Pluck the keen teeth from the fierce tiger's jaws,
And burn the long-liv'd phoenix in her blood;
Make glad and sorry seasons as thou fleets,
And do whate'er thou wilt, swift-footed Time,
To the wide world and all her fading sweets;
But I forbid thee one most heinous crime:—
Oh carve not with thy hours my love's fair brow,
Nor draw no lines there with thine antique pen;
Him in thy course untainted do allow
For beauty's pattern to succeeding men.
    Yet, do thy worst old Time: despite thy wrong,
    My love shall in my verse ever live young.

20

A woman's face with nature's own hand painted,
Hast thou, the master-mistress of my passion;
A woman's gentle heart, but not acquainted
With shifting change as is false women's fashion;
An eye more bright than theirs, less false in rolling,
Gilding the object whereupon it gazeth;
A man in hue all hues in his controlling,
Which steals men's eyes and women's souls amazeth.
And for a woman wert thou first created—
Till Nature as she wrought thee fell a-doting,
And by addition me of thee defeated,
By adding one thing to my purpose nothing.
   But since she prick'd thee out for women's pleasure,
   Mine be thy love and thy love's use their treasure.

MY GLASS shall not persuade me I am old
So long as youth and thou are of one date;
But when in thee time's furrows I behold
Then look I death my days should expiate:
For all the beauty that doth cover thee
Is but the seemly raiment of my heart,
Which in thy breast doth live, as thine in me,—
How can I then be elder than thou art?
Oh therefore, love, be of thyself so wary
As I not for myself but for thee will;
Bearing thy heart, which I will keep so chary
As tender nurse her babe from faring ill:

> Presume not on thy heart when mine is slain,
> Thou gav'st me thine not to give back again.

23

A s an unperfect actor on the stage,
Who with his fear is put besides his part,
Or some fierce thing replete with too much rage,
Whose strength's abundance weakens his own heart;
So I for fear of trust forget to say
The perfect ceremony of love's rite,
And in mine own love's strength seem to decay,
O'ercharg'd with burthen of mine own love's might:
Oh let my looks be then the eloquence
And dumb presagers of my speaking breast,
Who plead for love and look for recompense
More than that tongue that more hath more express'd:
    Oh learn to read what silent love hath writ;
    To hear with eyes belongs to love's fine wit.

MINE EYE hath play'd the painter and hath steeled
Thy beauty's form in table of my heart;
My body is the frame wherein 'tis held,
And perspective that is best painter's art—
For through the painter must you see his skill,
To find where your true image pictur'd lies,
Which in my bosom's shop is hanging still,
That hath his windows glazèd with thine eyes:
Now see what good turns eyes for eyes have done:—
Mine eyes have drawn thy shape, and thine for me
Are windows to my breast, wherethrough the sun
Delights to peep, to gaze therein on thee;
    Yet eyes this cunning want to grace their art,
    They draw but what they see, know not the heart.

26

L ORD OF my love, to whom in vassalage
 Thy merit hath my duty strongly knit,
To thee I send this written ambassage,
To witness duty, not to show my wit,—
Duty so great, which wit so poor as mine
May make seem bare, in wanting words to shew it,
But that I hope some good conceit of thine
In thy soul's thought all naked will bestow it,
Till whatsoever star that guides my moving,
Points on me graciously with fair aspect,
And puts apparel on my tatter'd loving
To show me worthy of thy sweet respect:
   Then may I dare to boast how I do love thee;—
   Till then, not show my head where thou mayst prove me.

WEARY WITH toil I haste me to my bed,
    The dear repose for limbs with travel tir'd;
But then begins a journey in my head
To work my mind when body's work's expired:
For then my thoughts, from far where I abide,
Intend a zealous pilgrimage to thee,
And keep my drooping eyelids open wide,
Looking on darkness which the blind do see:
Save that my soul's imaginary sight
Presents thy shadow to my sightless view,
Which like a jewel hung in ghastly night
Makes black night beauteous and her old face new.
    Lo, thus by day my limbs, by night my mind,
      For thee, and for myself, no quiet find.

28

How can I then return in happy plight
That am debarr'd the benefit of rest,
When day's oppression is not eas'd by night,
But day by night and night by day oppress'd,
And each, though enemies to other's reign,
Do in consent shake hands to torture me,
The one by toil, the other to complain
How far I toil, still farther off from thee?
I tell the day to please him thou art bright
And dost him grace when clouds do blot the heaven:
So flatter I the swart-complexion'd night
When sparkling stars twire not thou gild'st the even.
  But day doth daily draw my sorrows longer,
  And night doth nightly make grief's length seem stronger.

WHEN IN disgrace with Fortune and men's eyes,
 I all alone beweep my outcast state,
And trouble deaf heaven with my bootless cries,
And look upon myself and curse my fate—
Wishing me like to one more rich in hope,
Featur'd like him, like him with friends possess'd,
Desiring this man's art and that man's scope,
With what I most enjoy contented least;
Yet in these thoughts my self almost despising
Haply I think on thee, and then my state,
Like to the lark at break of day arising
From sullen earth, sings hymns at heaven's gate;
    For thy sweet love remembered such wealth brings
    That then I scorn to change my state with kings.

30

WHEN TO the sessions of sweet silent thought
   I summon up remembrance of things past,
I sigh the lack of many a thing I sought,
And with old woes new wail my dear time's waste:
Then can I drown an eye, unus'd to flow,
For precious friends hid in death's dateless night,
And weep afresh love's long since cancell'd woe,
And moan th'expense of many a vanish'd sight:
Then can I grieve at grievances foregone,
And heavily from woe to woe tell o'er
The sad account of fore-bemoanèd moan,
Which I new pay as if not paid before.
      But if the while I think on thee, dear friend,
      All losses are restor'd and sorrows end.

33

FULL MANY a glorious morning have I seen
Flatter the mountain tops with sovereign eye,
Kissing with golden face the meadows green,
Gilding pale streams with heavenly alchemy,—
Anon permit the basest clouds to ride
With ugly rack on his celestial face,
And from the forlorn world his visage hide,
Stealing unseen to west with this disgrace:
Even so my sun one early morn did shine,
With all triumphant splendour on my brow;
But out alack, he was but one hour mine—
The region cloud hath mask'd him from me now.
  Yet him for this my love no whit disdaineth;
  Suns of the world may stain, when heaven's sun staineth.

34

WHY DIDST thou promise such a beauteous day,
    And make me travel forth without my cloak,
To let base clouds o'ertake me in my way,
Hiding thy bravery in their rotten smoke?
'Tis not enough that through the cloud thou break
To dry the rain on my storm-beaten face,
For no man well of such a salve can speak
That heals the wound and cures not the disgrace:
Nor can thy shame give physic to my grief;
Though thou repent, yet I have still the loss:
Th'offender's sorrow lends but weak relief
To him that bears the strong offence's cross.
    Ah, but those tears are pearl which thy love sheds;
    And they are rich, and ransom all ill deeds.

35

No more be griev'd at that which thou hast done:
Roses have thorns, and silver fountains mud,
Clouds and eclipses stain both moon and sun,
And loathsome canker lives in sweetest bud;
All men make faults, and even I in this,
Authorizing thy trespass with compare,
My self corrupting salving thy amiss,
Excusing their sins more than their sins are;
For to thy sensual fault I bring in sense—
Thy adverse party is thy advocate—
And 'gainst myself a lawful plea commence:
Such civil war is in my love and hate
    That I an accessary needs must be
    To that sweet thief which sourly robs from me.

36

L ET ME confess that we two must be twain
Although our undivided loves are one:
So shall those blots that do with me remain
Without thy help by me be borne alone.
In our two loves there is but one respect,
Though in our lives a separable spite,
Which, though it alter not love's sole effect,
Yet doth it steal sweet hours from love's delight.
I may not evermore acknowledge thee,
Lest my bewailèd guilt should do thee shame;
Nor thou with public kindness honour me,
Unless thou take that honour from thy name:
    But do not so; I love thee in such sort
    As, thou being mine, mine is thy good report.

TAKE ALL my loves, my love, yea, take them all:
  What hast thou then more than thou hadst before?
No love, my love, that thou mayst true love call—
All mine was thine, before thou hadst this more.
Then if for my love thou my love receivest,
I cannot blame thee, for my love thou usest,—
But yet be blam'd, if thou this self deceivest
By wilful taste of what thy self refusest.
I do forgive thy robbery, gentle thief,
Although thou steal thee all my poverty:
And yet love knows it is a greater grief
To bear love's wrong, than hate's known injury.
    Lascivious grace, in whom all ill well shows,
    Kill me with spites, yet we must not be foes.

43

WHEN MOST I wink, then do mine eyes best see,
   For all the day they view things unrespected;
But when I sleep, in dreams they look on thee,
And darkly bright are bright in dark directed.
Then thou whose shadow shadows doth make bright,
How would thy shadow's form form happy show
To the clear day with thy much clearer light,
When to unseeing eyes thy shade shines so!
How would, I say, mine eyes be blessèd made
By looking on thee in the living day,
When in dead night thy fair imperfect shade
Through heavy sleep on sightless eyes doth stay!
   All days are nights to see till I see thee,
   And nights bright days when dreams do show thee me.

MINE EYE and heart are at a mortal war,
How to divide the conquest of thy sight;
Mine eye my heart thy picture's sight would bar,—
My heart, mine eye the freedom of that right:
My heart doth plead that thou in him dost lie—
A closet never pierc'd with crystal eyes;
But the defendant doth that plea deny,
And says in him thy fair appearance lies.
To 'cide this title is impannellèd
A quest of thoughts, all tenants to the heart,
And by their verdict is determinèd
The clear eye's moiety and the dear heart's part,
 As thus: mine eye's due is thine outward part,
 And my heart's right, thine inward love of heart.

NOT MARBLE, nor the gilded monuments
Of princes, shall outlive this powerful rhyme;
But you shall shine more bright in these contents
Than unswept stone besmear'd with sluttish time.
When wasteful war shall statues overturn,
And broils root out the work of masonry,
Nor Mars his sword nor war's quick fire shall burn
The living record of your memory.
'Gainst death, and all oblivious enmity
Shall you pace forth; your praise shall still find room
Even in the eyes of all posterity
That wear this world out to the ending doom.
  So, till the judgment that yourself arise,
  You live in this, and dwell in lovers' eyes.

60

L IKE AS the waves make towards the pebbled shore,
So do our minutes hasten to their end;
Each changing place with that which goes before
In sequent toil all forwards do contend.
Nativity, once in the main of light,
Crawls to maturity, wherewith being crown'd,
Crooked eclipses 'gainst his glory fight,
And Time that gave doth now his gift confound.
Time doth transfix the flourish set on youth,
And delves the parallels in beauty's brow,
Feeds on the rarities of nature's truth;
And nothing stands but for his scythe to mow.
  And yet to times in hope my verse shall stand
  Praising thy worth, despite his cruel hand.

73

THAT TIME of year thou mayst in me behold
When yellow leaves, or none, or few, do hang
Upon those boughs which shake against the cold,
Bare ruin'd choirs, where late the sweet birds sang:
In me thou see'st the twilight of such day
As after sunset fadeth in the west,
Which by and by black night doth take away,
Death's second self that seals up all in rest:
In me thou see'st the glowing of such fire
That on the ashes of his youth doth lie
As the death-bed whereon it must expire,
Consum'd with that which it was nourish'd by:
   This thou perceiv'st, which makes thy love more strong
   To love that well, which thou must leave ere long.

Was it the proud full sail of his great verse,
  Bound for the prize of all-too-precious you,
That did my ripe thoughts in my brain inhearse,
Making their tomb the womb wherein they grew?
Was it his spirit, by spirits taught to write
Above a mortal pitch, that struck me dead?
No, neither he, nor his compeers by night
Giving him aid, my verse astonishèd.
He, nor that affable familiar ghost
Which nightly gulls him with intelligence,
As victors of my silence cannot boast,—
I was not sick of any fear from thence:
  But when your countenance fill'd up his line,
  Then lack'd I matter; that enfeebl'd mine.

94

THEY THAT have power to hurt and will do none,
   That do not do the thing they most do show,
Who moving others are themselves as stone,
Unmovèd, cold, and to temptation slow—
They rightly do inherit heaven's graces,
And husband nature's riches from expense;
They are the lords and owners of their faces,
Others but stewards of their excellence.
The summer's flower is to the summer sweet,
Though to itself it only live and die;
But if that flower with base infection meet,
The basest weed outbraves his dignity:
   For sweetest things turn sourest by their deeds;
   Lilies that fester smell far worse than weeds.

95

How sweet and lovely dost thou make the shame
Which like a canker in the fragrant rose
Doth spot the beauty of thy budding name!
Oh, in what sweets dost thou thy sins enclose!
That tongue that tells the story of thy days,
Making lascivious comments on thy sport,
Cannot dispraise, but in a kind of praise;
Naming thy name blesses an ill report.
Oh, what a mansion have those vices got
Which for their habitation chose out thee!—
Where beauty's veil doth cover every blot
And all things turns to fair that eyes can see.
  Take heed, dear heart, of this large privilege:
  The hardest knife ill us'd doth lose his edge.

98

Fʀᴏᴍ ʏᴏᴜ have I been absent in the spring,
When proud-pied April, dress'd in all his trim,
Hath put a spirit of youth in every thing,
That heavy Saturn laugh'd and leapt with him.
Yet nor the lays of birds, nor the sweet smell
Of different flowers in odour and in hue,
Could make me any summer's story tell,
Or from their proud lap pluck them where they grew:
Nor did I wonder at the lily's white,
Nor praise the deep vermilion in the rose;
They were but sweet, but figures of delight
Drawn after you, you pattern of all those.
   Yet seemed it winter still; and, you away,
   As with your shadow I with these did play.

104

To me, fair friend, you never can be old,
  For as you were when first your eye I ey'd,
Such seems your beauty still: three winters cold
Have from the forests shook three summers' pride,
Three beauteous springs to yellow autumn turn'd,
In process of the seasons have I seen,
Three April perfumes in three hot Junes burn'd,
Since first I saw you fresh, which yet are green.
Ah! yet doth beauty like a dial hand
Steal from his figure and no pace perceiv'd;
So your sweet hue, which methinks still doth stand,
Hath motion, and mine eye may be deceiv'd—
    For fear of which hear this, thou age unbred:
    Ere you were born was beauty's summer dead.

WHEN IN the chronicle of wasted time
  I see descriptions of the fairest wights,
And beauty making beautiful old rhyme
In praise of ladies dead and lovely knights,
Then in the blazon of sweet beauty's best—
Of hand, of foot, of lip, of eye, of brow—
I see their antique pen would have express'd
Even such a beauty as you master now:
So all their praises are but prophecies
Of this our time, all you prefiguring;
And for they look'd but with divining eyes
They had not skill enough your worth to sing:
    For we which now behold these present days
    Have eyes to wonder, but lack tongues to praise.

Not mine own fears, nor the prophetic soul
Of the wide world dreaming on things to come
Can yet the lease of my true love control,
Suppos'd as forfeit to a confin'd doom.
The mortal moon hath her eclipse endur'd,
And the sad augurs mock their own presage;
Incertainties now crown themselves assur'd,
And peace proclaims olives of endless age.
Now with the drops of this most balmy time
My love looks fresh; and Death to me subscribes,
Since spite of him I'll live in this poor rhyme
While he insults o'er dull and speechless tribes:
   And thou in this shalt find thy monument
   When tyrants' crests and tombs of brass are spent.

109

OH NEVER say that I was false of heart,
Though absence seem'd my flame to qualify!
As easy might I from my self depart
As from my soul, which in thy breast doth lie;—
That is my home of love: if I have rang'd,
Like him that travels, I return again;
Just to the time, not with the time exchanged,
So that myself bring water for my stain.
Never believe, though in my nature reign'd,
All frailties that besiege all kinds of blood,
That it could so preposterously be stain'd,
To leave for nothing all thy sum of good—
   For nothing this wide universe I call,
   Save thou my rose: in it thou art my all.

L ET ME not to the marriage of true minds
Admit impediments: love is not love
Which alters when it alteration finds,
Or bends with the remover to remove.
Oh no! it is an ever-fixèd mark,
That looks on tempests and is never shaken;
It is the star to every wandering bark,
Whose worth's unknown although his height be taken.
Love's not Time's fool, though rosy lips and cheeks
Within his bending sickle's compass come;
Love alters not with his brief hours and weeks,
But bears it out even to the edge of doom.
    If this be error and upon me prov'd,
    I never writ, nor no man ever lov'd.

L IKE AS, to make our appetites more keen,
  With eager compounds we our palate urge;
As to prevent our maladies unseen
We sicken to shun sickness when we purge:
Even so, being full of your ne'er cloying sweetness,
To bitter sauces did I frame my feeding;
And, sick of welfare, found a kind of meetness
To be diseas'd ere that there was true needing.
Thus policy in love, t'anticipate
The ills that were not, grew to faults assur'd,
And brought to medicine a healthful state
Which, rank of goodness, would by ill be cured;
  But thence I learn and find the lesson true,
  Drugs poison him that so fell sick of you.

IN THE old age black was not counted fair,
Or if it were, it bore not beauty's name;
But now is black beauty's successive heir,
And beauty slander'd with a bastard shame:
For since each hand hath put on Nature's power,
Fairing the foul with Art's false borrow'd face,
Sweet beauty hath no name, no holy bower,
But is profan'd, if not lives in disgrace.
Therefore my mistress' eyes are raven black,
Her eyes so suited, and they mourners seem
At such who, not born fair, no beauty lack,
Slandering creation with a false esteem:
  Yet so they mourn becoming of their woe,
  That every tongue says beauty should look so.

128

How OFT, when thou, my music, music play'st
Upon that blessèd wood whose motion sounds
With thy sweet fingers, when thou gently sway'st
The wiry concord that mine ear confounds,
Do I envy those jacks that nimble leap,
To kiss the tender inward of thy hand,
Whilst my poor lips, which should that harvest reap,
At the wood's boldness by thee blushing stand!
To be so tickled they would change their state
And situation with those dancing chips,
O'er whom thy fingers walk with gentle gait,
Making dead wood more blest than living lips.
  Since saucy jacks so happy are in this,
  Give them thy fingers, me thy lips to kiss.

TH' EXPENSE of spirit in a waste of shame
  Is lust in action; and till action, lust
Is perjur'd, murderous, bloody, full of blame,
Savage, extreme, rude, cruel, not to trust;
Enjoy'd no sooner but despisèd straight;
Past reason hunted; and no sooner had,
Past reason hated, as a swallow'd bait,
On purpose laid to make the taker mad—
Mad in pursuit, and in possession so;
Had, having, and in quest to have, extreme;
A bliss in proof; and proved, a very woe;
Before, a joy proposed; behind a dream.
  All this the world well knows; yet none knows well
  To shun the heaven that leads men to this hell.

130

M Y MISTRESS' eyes are nothing like the sun;
Coral is far more red than her lips' red:
If snow be white, why then her breasts are dun;
If hairs be wires, black wires grow on her head.
I have seen roses damask'd, red and white,
But no such roses see I in her cheeks;
And in some perfumes is there more delight
Than in the breath that from my mistress reeks:
I love to hear her speak, yet well I know
That music hath a far more pleasing sound;
I grant I never saw a goddess go,—
My mistress, when she walks, treads on the ground.
  And yet by heaven I think my love as rare
  As any she belied with false compare.

133

BESHREW THAT heart that makes my heart to groan
For that deep wound it gives my friend and me!
Is't not enough to torture me alone,
But slave to slavery my sweet'st friend must be?
Me from myself thy cruel eye hath taken,
And my next self thou harder hast engross'd:
Of him, myself, and thee I am forsaken,—
A torment thrice threefold thus to be cross'd.
Prison my heart in thy steel bosom's ward,
But then my friend's heart let my poor heart bail;
Whoe'er keeps me, let my heart be his guard;
Thou canst not then use rigour in my jail.
  And yet thou wilt; for I, being pent in thee,
  Perforce am thine, and all that is in me.

134

So, NOW I have confessed that he is thine,
And I my self am mortgag'd to thy will,
My self I'll forfeit, so that other mine
Thou wilt restore to be my comfort still.
But thou wilt not, nor he will not be free,
For thou art covetous, and he is kind;
He learn'd but surety-like to write for me
Under that bond that him as fast doth bind.
The statute of thy beauty thou wilt take,
Thou usurer, that put'st forth all to use,
And sue a friend came debtor for my sake;
So him I lose through my unkind abuse.
   Him have I lost; thou hast both him and me:
   He pays the whole, and yet am I not free.

138

WHEN MY love swears that she is made of truth,
I do believe her, though I know she lies,
That she might think me some untutor'd youth,
Unlearnèd in the world's false subtleties.
Thus vainly thinking that she thinks me young,
Although she knows my days are past the best,
Simply I credit her false-speaking tongue:
On both sides thus is simple truth suppress'd.
But wherefore says she not she is unjust?
And wherefore say not I that I am old?
Oh, love's best habit is in seeming trust,
And age in love loves not to have years told.
    Therefore I lie with her, and she with me,
    And in our faults by lies we flatter'd be.

144

Two loves I have, of comfort and despair,
Which like two spirits do suggest me still:
The better angel is a man right fair,
The worser spirit a woman colour'd ill.
To win me soon to hell, my female evil
Tempteth my better angel from my side,
And would corrupt my saint to be a devil,
Wooing his purity with her foul pride.
And whether that my angel be turn'd fiend,
Suspect I may, yet not directly tell;
But being both from me, both to each friend,
I guess one angel in another's hell:
   Yet this shall I ne'er know, but live in doubt
   Till my bad angel fire my good one out.

147

M<small>Y LOVE</small> is as a fever, longing still
For that which longer nurseth the disease,
Feeding on that which doth preserve the ill,
Th'uncertain sickly appetite to please.
My reason, the physician to my love,
Angry that his prescriptions are not kept,
Hath left me, and I desperate now approve
Desire is death, which physic did except.
Past cure I am now reason is past care,
And frantic-mad with evermore unrest;
My thoughts and my discourse as madmen's are,
At random from the truth, vainly express'd;
  For I have sworn thee fair, and thought thee bright,
  Who art as black as hell, as dark as night.

L ove is too young to know what conscience is,—
Yet who knows not conscience is born of love?
Then, gentle cheater, urge not my amiss,
Lest guilty of my faults thy sweet self prove:
For, thou betraying me, I do betray
My nobler part to my gross body's treason;
My soul doth tell my body that he may
Triumph in love: flesh stays no farther reason,
But rising at thy name doth point out thee
As his triumphant prize. Proud of this pride,
He is contented thy poor drudge to be,
To stand in thy affairs, fall by thy side.
  No want of conscience hold it that I call
  Her 'love', for whose dear love I rise and fall.

153

CUPID LAID by his brand and fell asleep.
A maid of Dian's this advantage found,
And his love-kindling fire did quickly steep
In a cold valley-fountain of that ground;
Which borrow'd from this holy fire of Love,
A dateless lively heat, still to endure,
And grew a seething bath which yet men prove
Against strange maladies a sovereign cure.
But at my mistress' eye Love's brand new-fir'd,
The boy for trial needs would touch my breast;
I, sick withal, the help of bath desir'd,
And thither hied, a sad distemper'd guest;
  But found no cure: the bath for my help lies
  Where Cupid got new fire—my mistress' eyes.